MUMMY EATERS

African POETRY BOOK SERIES

Series editor: Kwame Dawes

MUMMY EATERS

Sherry Shenoda

Foreword by Kwame Dawes

University of Nebraska Press / Lincoln

The University of Nebraska Press is part of a land-
grant institution with campuses and programs on the
past, present, and future homelands of the Pawnee,
Ponca, Otoe-Missouria, Omaha, Dakota, Lakota, Kaw,
Cheyenne, and Arapaho Peoples, as well as those of the
relocated Ho-Chunk, Sac and Fox, and Iowa Peoples.

♾

The African Poetry Book Series is operated by
the African Poetry Book Fund. The APBF was
established in 2012 with initial support from
philanthropists Laura and Robert F. X. Sillerman.
The founding director of the African Poetry Book
Fund is Kwame Dawes, Holmes University Professor
and Glenna Luschei Editor of *Prairie Schooner*.

Library of Congress Cataloging-in-Publication Data
Names: Shenoda, Sherry, author. | Dawes, Kwame
Senu Neville, 1962– writer of foreword.
Title: Mummy eaters / Sherry Shenoda ;
foreword by Kwame Dawes.
Description: Lincoln : University of Nebraska
Press, [2022] | Series: African poetry book
series | Includes bibliographical references.
Identifiers: LCCN 2022008572
ISBN 9781496232540 (paperback)
ISBN 9781496234100 (epub)
ISBN 9781496234117 (pdf)
Subjects: BISAC: POETRY / African | LCGFT: Poetry.
Classification: LCC PS3619.H45385
M86 2022 | DDC 811/.6—dc23
LC record available at https://
lccn.loc.gov/2022008572

Set in Garamond Premier by Laura Buis.

For Nadra, Fouziya, and Malaka, queens.

May we live and remember.

CONTENTS

FOREWORD

KWAME DAWES

Mummy Eaters is first and foremost a work of profound sentiment and sheer beauty. Sherry Shenoda's skill as a poet is hard to ignore, and this sophistication is marked only by the ambition of her subject. The "Invocation" that opens the collection presents us with the scale and scope of her vision, which manages the remarkable balance of personal sentiment, intellectual inquisitiveness, and an admirable understanding of the history of her people. It also establishes a clear hierarchy of cultural value that is disruptive to persistent colonizing logic. The refrain in "Invocation" is "plant me"—a prayer for belonging, for grounding, and in the case of the collection, for a spiritual foundation that stretches from the Ethiopian Highlands through the "lower Nubia" to the streets of Alexandria. It is increasingly clear that Shenoda is tracing her own migratory biographical and ancestral path, which will eventually embrace the Golden Gate Bridge and the Empire State Building of her new home in the United States:

> Would that I could plant in handfuls of seeds
> myself offered in peace.
>
> Plant me in the Ethiopian Highlands before
> the Renaissance Dam, in lower Nubia before
>
> the Aswan Dam, in the streets of Alexandria
> between the mob and the body of Hypatia,

between decay and loss of knowledge, plant me
on the steps of the Library of Alexandria.

Plant me between every tongue that prays, O God,
the Great and Eternal, and every tongue that prays,

In the Name of God, the Most Merciful, plant me
between the Heights and the Bank,

between the Golden Gate, Gate of Mercy,
and the Gate of Repentance, plant me.

Between the Golden Gate Bridge and the
Empire State Building, broken heart land

of my rebel country, plant me until we bud
forgiveness, the ground hallowed,

and from lamentation our song swells,
from dark earth, an ascendant praise.
    ("Sunflowers of Fukushima")

The collection opens with a moment of transportation that introduces us
to the core theme of the work—the capacity to consider the present moment
through a prism that can reach as far back into history as 1339 BC, and yet
manage to engage that period and those individuals and their bodies through
the rich and evocative language of the senses and the physical body. Shenoda's
present voice is shaped and defined by a long line of women, and in this imag-
inative act, she locates the female self as constantly present:

My heart remembers skipped beats to cobra danger
slithering and scattering grain mice.

I can almost smell heady sweet
blue lotus, the scent of Resurrection.

Now my eyes are opened.
Now my mouth is opened.
I am racing toward Life.
    ("Ancestor Opening of the Mouth: A Daughter's Long Wail")

The poem is, at once, a persona poem, spoken in the voice of the spirit of a mummified body, and yet, through the function of the first person, a lyric poem in which the poet imagines herself as "long-memoried" and able to "remember" several thousand years in the past. Throughout the collection, Shenoda enacts this necessary engagement with history and myth in a way that makes it profoundly present and relevant to the current moment. The rituals of mummification are elemental to the present moment, and in this, most African of senses, the past of the ancestors is an acute present. In "Descendant Ponders the Rising Cost of Dying," Shenoda locates the poet as the descendant, and her moving concerns about the rituals of dying in the present moment are set in relief by her reflections into the past. The poem opens with a critique of ancient Egyptian society:

For the family of Pharaoh: several coffins.
The rich can afford to die several times,
or even, it turns out, just once.

This wry observation is set against her experience as a doctor:

What kind of graceless space
do we live in,
where the dead remain unburied,
until the living raise enough money
to unlock the ground?

Shenoda repeats this genius of exploring the urgent history of a world that remains as complex as it has ever been. I describe it as genius because her craft, her skill at creating poems that employ clear and sophisticated syntax to allow her to make intellectual leaps and emotional shifts that traverse the personal, the political, the spiritual, and the historical, is what shines through here.

One of the most powerful sequences in the collection demonstrates this quality with elegance and urgency. The sequence, "How to Silence," is a study of the wounds created by all manner of silencing, whether political, religious, linguistic, cultural, or sexual. In the final poem in that movement, "How to Silence IV: Arabic Lessons," we witness Shenoda at her finest. I quote the poem its entirety here, as something of a trailer for the collection. Shenoda addresses her sister in this poem. The effect is an intimacy that is filled with vulnerability and generosity. We are being allowed into the sacred place of family. The poem begins with a deeply personal remembering, a moment of domestic disquiet:

> Sister, when our mother woke after surgery,
> breast abscess excised, unable to nurse,
>
> nearly losing her life, Baba across oceans,
> her Muslim sisters divvied her call shifts.
>
> When she woke scared, one sat beside her
> rocking and praying the Koran.

And then the view expands, moving from the intimacy of family to the broader dynamics of a culture that has been shaped by a distinct history. The Coptic experience is understood with clarity here, and has to be accounted for, even as the poem remains wholly personal in its urgency and sentiment:

> Hurt ones entreat me to tell tales of tongue slashers,
> permits to fix toilets in crumbling churches, permits

requiring presidential signatures. *To relieve ourselves,*
Presidential signatures, they wail.

They tell tales of hands that rip crosses from necks,
spray backs of churches with bullets.

Those are not tales, they are true but
truer still and more urgent is the tale of our mother.

In the final address, we come to understand the urgency that undergirds this
effort to cross the grand divides of dogma and religion. The sister who speaks
ventures toward a posture of compromise, a posture that seeks to "chant of
God" despite the profound, but ultimately, superficially manifested divides that
have come to consume this family. Shenoda is not willing to leave the matter
at the point of interrogation. Instead, the poem ends with a declaration, an
aspiration for a certain transcendent unity:

I ask you, What need have we of persecuted minorities
in one country calling out persecuted minorities

in another country? And would it help if hatred
bred hatred, or instead of giving airtime to cross rippers,

could we pray ourselves awake chanting of God
in whatever tongue left to us? I will rock over you,

sister (whatever you do with your hair:
braid it, curl it, cover it, or shave it),

rock over you chanting *Ekowab*.
You will rock over me chanting *Bismillah*.

And we will rock and chant together
until these nations find their tongues, until the soil

black once more and the River twist liberated,
dancing into the mouth of the sea.
    ("How to Silence IV: Arabic Lessons")

This is compelling poetry that takes us from the intimacy of family to the political complications of history to an expansive sisterhood. The imposition of the Arabic tongue on a Coptic people is understood with wry humor and fitting irony: "I ask you, What need have we of persecuted minorities / in one country calling out persecuted minorities // in another country?" Yet, for Shenoda, there is the quest for a certain hope in the path toward unity that is built on the shared respect for the different tongues, which become symbols of whole civilizations, cultures, and faiths. For her, the hope of voices chanting together is captured in the image of fecundity and fertility—the soil black with the moisture of the "River" that is "dancing into the mouth of the sea."

As the ninth winner of the annual Sillerman Prize for African Poetry, *Mummy Eaters* continues the groundbreaking trend that has characterized each new volume of poetry published in this series. Shenoda dismantles the cliché of mummification nurtured by Western culture by revealing an intimate and nuanced engagement with Egyptian civilization and Egypt's complex and evolving culture.

ACKNOWLEDGMENTS

My debts are many, but in trying, I send love to my beloved sisters Veronica, Sandra, Marina, Laura, Helena, and Anna, who encourage and ennoble my creative life.

Much respect and gratitude to Kwame Dawes for his kindness and humor throughout the editing process. This book is immeasurably strengthened by his wisdom. Haley Mendlik, thank you for your equally generous lead eye on the manuscript. To the staff at the African Poetry Book Fund and University of Nebraska Press: thank you for making this work possible. A special thank you to Margie Blevins, for naming me a writer, and to Matthew Shenoda and Mahtem Shiferaw for encouraging me to try, and try again.

Mom, Dad, Michael—love inexpressible, and only uttered slant. Basil and Tobias, for their patience, and Andrew, as always, first and last.

INTRODUCTION

Beginning in the reign of Akhenaten, considered a heretic pharaoh, here is an imagined path from his assertion that the Sun-disk was a manifestation of God, through colonialism in Egypt, to the modern Coptic tradition. The mythology of the ancient Egyptians is oriented toward Resurrection through the preservation of the human body in mummification. This reverence for the human body as sacred matter and a pathway to eternal life is examined through the lens of the practice of mummy eating. In the sixteenth and seventeenth centuries Europeans ate Egyptian human remains as medicine. They used Egyptian human remains as paper, paint, and fertilizer. Today Egyptian human remains are displayed in museums. Much of this collection is written as a call and response, in the Coptic tradition, between an imagined ancestor, one of the daughters of the house of Akhenaten, and the author as descendant.

MUMMY EATERS

Sunflowers of Fukushima

Invocation

Monk Koyn Abe gifts seeds
in a land desolate with exile.

These broad-faced sun worshippers stand golden
crowned eight cubits high in peaceful armies

to sip toxic radiation from abused soil,
hyperaccumulate poison, serve, and be uprooted.

Would that I could plant in handfuls of seeds
myself offered in peace.

Plant me in the Ethiopian Highlands before
the Renaissance Dam, in lower Nubia before

the Aswan Dam, in the streets of Alexandria
between the mob and the body of Hypatia,

between decay and loss of knowledge, plant me
on the steps of the Library of Alexandria.

Plant me between every tongue that prays, O God,
the Great and Eternal, and every tongue that prays,

In the Name of God, the Most Merciful, plant me
between the Heights and the Bank,

between the Golden Gate, Gate of Mercy,
and the Gate of Repentance, plant me.

Between the Golden Gate Bridge and the
Empire State Building, broken heart land

of my rebel country, plant me until we bud
forgiveness, the ground hallowed,

and from lamentation our song swells,
from dark earth, an ascendant praise.

I

Ancestor Opening of the Mouth

A Daughter's Long Wail

1339 BC, Eighteenth Dynasty, Egypt/Kemet

Acacia flowers shield my breast.
I can almost smell tang of garlic

in meat they press into my mouth.
My first taste of love at mother's breast.

The last now, of spiced wild gazelle.
May she aid me to run like the River.

I am Meritaten-tasherit, Beloved of Aten, the Younger.
My life rang of gold, lapis lazuli, hymns to Aten.

Crowned in carnelian and gold,
draped in youngest flax spun to linen,

I carried the sistrum behind my mother and sisters.
Then plague. My mother's long wail.

Forty days have I lain in natron,
alone for my own preservation.

Now my eyes are opened.
Now my mouth is opened to

dark sweetness of date, ruby pomegranate,
brine of olive, smoke of River-fish.

My eyes can almost see neck hair rise on my hound,
slide of crocodile hide on River-banks.

My hands long for my cat's purring warmth
beneath my palm, my sister's soft coos.

My ears crane to the song of harp, sharp
clash of cymbals, and flute mischief.

My scalp craves the caress of dry wind,
stinging sand whipping my skin.

My heart remembers skipped beats to cobra danger
slithering and scattering grain mice.

I can almost smell heady sweet
blue lotus, the scent of Resurrection.

Now my eyes are opened.
Now my mouth is opened.
I am racing toward Life.

Aftermath

A Mother's Long Wail

May the hand of Re steady the hand of the priest,
to preserve her beloved face to face life beyond life.

May she recognize her-*self*,
her soul in the Field of Reeds.
May they sway on a mild breeze before her.

What now must I do with this Absence left behind?
This life cratered in her shape?

Absence of her has become a presence.
Absence lies down, rises up.
Absence sleeps, soft-cheeked, curled in her bed.

The room is still, expectant.
I will give her clothes away, but not yet.
Absence wears them. Her soft linen.
Absence outlines her eyes in dark malachite.

Like my breasts that leaked milk
in mute grief after the daughter born still,
I leak now in mute grief, though the priests remind me
she is alive, there, through the aperture of grief.

I look up expecting her face in the doorway,
but it is empty, again and again it is empty,
save for the Absence.

Absence unaccustomed to the light,
presses heavy on my chest at night,
of a body that carried, gave birth
to a life ripped from me in pain,
twice.

Mummification

Early Lessons

I
Brain
    Wash, purify,
    rub with sacred oil,
    hook through nose,
    discard that for which
    no use could be found.
    —all thoughts fly—

II
The Tricky Part
    for the priests was of course
    to get the brain out without
    distorting her face. Like plastic
    surgery but the highest-stakes
    nose job of all time. Instead
    of ruined selfies, a soul
    unable to recognize her-*self.*

III
Lungs
    While heart opposite feather
    awaits judgment,
    how does spirit hold
    her breath?
    Do lungs—jarred
    beside a dark sarcophagus—
    catch?

IV

Wadi el Natroun

Slice along left flank,
organs in alabaster jars.

How does it feel, hollowed out,
filled with natron and left alone
under the heat of the desert sun
forty days
for your own preservation?

Young Macarius the Great, Lamp of the Desert,
drove a camel carrying natron, he carrying Wisdom
before cherubim took him by hand into Shi-het,
inner desert where hearts are measured,
as Anubis of the Ancients took Ka
by hand to offer his heart to be measured.

Alone forty days in the wilderness.
Alone for your own preservation.

V

Heart

Seat of intelligence and memory.
House of emotion, nest now, undisturbed
in this cradle of chest and ark of ribs.
Rest after your toils and wait
scarab-protected
to be handed over in judgement, but pray,

Do not stand
as a witness against me.

From Mummification to the Incarnation

We who fret and toil, plumb the depths of soil.
We who worry and wonder over the ancient problem:
And what of the body?
Soma sema, wrote Plato, *the body, a tomb.*

We who wear this curse-crowned garment of sinew and secrets ask,
Is it holy or heresy to hate the house that holds the soul?
Heresy as old as Cain, who found heavy on his hands
a body to be dealt with, a delicate but weighty matter.

We who bear up, heavy with our body burden
like a staggering line of pallbearers.
We who grasp to buy back youth, bounce back
after babies and ward off old age like the coming of plague.
We who slim down to take up less space, modify
our bodies to fit our garments, ask,

Was God's prophet not sent to prophesy
over a field of bones, dry as dust?
Did the Resurrection not begin
at the moment of Incarnation, in sacred matter?

From death to entombment, the Ancients labored
seventy days with slow-moving reverent hands,
packing natron, green herbs, preserving all they could,
especially the beloved visage. Witness.
We who behold the body, in glory, prepared for Resurrection.

Descendant Ponders the Rising Cost of Dying

I

For the family of Pharaoh: several coffins.
The rich can afford to die several times,
or even, it turns out, just once.

II

There was a man begging today
at the side of the road
for funeral donations.

"One, two, or five hundred dollars,
any amount helps."

III

What they don't tell you,
when you go to medical school,
is that among the fever, croup,
diaper rashes, ear infections,

you have to stop everything

to call the funeral director
and plead on behalf of your patient's brother,
shot on the front doorstep,
three weeks dead.

What kind of graceless space
do we live in,
where the dead remain unburied,
until the living raise enough money
to unlock the ground?

Makeup

On a mummy makeup is applied
when the body petrifies.
In life she wears Bastet eyes, bowed brows over
full mouth and dark swaying braids.

In life she wears milk and honey face masks,
spice oil rubbed into her skin, sugared hair.
Unguents and perfumes wait in calcite jars.
Ochre red lips, rich green malachite mixed in
animal fat, dipped and lined with ivory-handled
sticks carved in the likeness of Hathor.
In life she paints her eyes against danger,
against Sun-glare with kohl and shadow.

In death her skin is tree bark.
She wears false eyes, a false face, a likeness
unlike her. How will she recognize her-*self*?
A priest covers her face covered
in resin with makeup and one
questions the necessity. One
always questions the necessity.

Race against Time I

I

A final gift, what any loving family would provide,
provided they had the means. A scroll,
personal Book of the Dead
tucked beneath her mummy's hands.
Spells to cross by coffin to the sky goddess Nut,
to Duat, to Heaven by Night.

II

The poor cannot buy the same time.
It is said they mummified naturally,

buried their dead, no less loved,
in linen, buried in hot dry sand.

Let the desert sun do its worst-best.
It is said sometimes they were better

preserved than the rich.

Shabti, Ushabti

"Answerer"

Small servants wear her face,
ready to answer, *Here I Am!*

on her behalf in the afterlife,
to spare her spirit manual labor.

In the flesh Ancestor's hands never hefted hoe or pick,
never lifted a scythe, but now in death,

this legion swells with life, to serve Osiris
in her stead, an essential army.

Ready to stand in her place, to face danger
on her behalf, till and furrow fields.

The more she can afford, the more of her time
she can spend in leisure, the more she can

buy back. Needless to say, the poor could not afford,
even in the afterlife, to not work. This host

announces her consequence by proxy,
a ready anaphora on their stony lips.

Descendant Ponders Space

Of Cairo's millions,
a multitude live in the cemeteries,
in sepulchers, with
the quietest of neighbors.

There is more space for them there
with the dead
than in the Victorious City
with the living.

Two or three times a year
we go to visit my grandparents
and the occupants make us *shai*,
assure us that all is well,
that they are taking care of things,
and that our dead are at peace.

And every fifty years
the bodies of the dead
will be consolidated

to make

space

for the bodies of the living.

Ancestor Dreams of the River Nile by a Dark Gate

West of the River Nile death-side
they bury me awaiting Eastern-life.

In sycomore fig shade I wait and pray
time settle an aloe on mother's heart.

It feels long and long as long
as the inundation, longer even,

bookended by longing and memory,
winding as the cataracts curve.

I float in sediment of memory,
time fragments of bedload.

My heart knows no fear of hippopotamus
flicking dark water from her ears. Instead,

I fear forgetting the demons' names,
sitting stranded by a dark gate for eternity.

Lend me, gazelle, your fleet hooves,
wise eagle eye, clever fingers of baboon,

stealth of cat, agility of mongoose,
flight of falcon, strike of shrew.

I seek the Field of Reeds, the blue lotus.
Bring the cobra. I do not fear him.

Kemet, Nile

I. Akhet: Flooding
Mending, tending, temple building.
Patient praying, but now in Aswan,
a High Dam.

In absence of floodwaters we still
ebb and flow to phantom inundations.

II. Peret: Growing
Skyscrapers root and crop instead of
once-black kemet, that rich black
fragrant loam which sprouted gold and grain.

The basket of her bread, grain that fed
armies of Alexander,
that fed a nation, that fed
many nations, or else why
the repetitive subjugations?

Fertile soil now ploughed and seeded
to feed foreign appetites.

III. Shemu: Harvest
Sickle down Progress,
that brass-bellied god
aloft like grain,
mark chaff,
what remains.
Lengthen our spines
against the next inundation.

Descendants, in Memory of Our Family Farm

Baba tells of walls three feet
thick with Nile mud and wheat chaff,
unearthed from wooden molds and baked
weeks in a furnace of desert sun.

At dusk my recent ancestors gather,
bring forth baskets of oranges, tamarind,
peanuts and figs, sweet dates, and split
melons round a corn-husk fire.

They spin stories, one uncle after another,
whatever comes to mind, while children sit rapt,
light glinting off ivory teeth and golden skin,
until the fruit runs out or the kerosene

lamps dim, or Ami says *y'alla*. Children
tuck in beside Aunt Hoda, Hosniya, Folla,
and Fouziya to fall asleep in deep evening,
until the morning cock wakes the farm.

Now harvesting of Nile mud, kemet
of the Inundation, that rich loamy silt,
long disappeared with the High Dam,
has become illegal, the old ways outlawed.

In Egypt a citizen may not
dig up the earth of her own land
to bake an earthen dwelling
to shelter her children from the sun.

Gone the farm and the Aunts and Ami.
Gone the old Tongue root-slashed.
Gone the old Language memory-faded.
Gone the black fertility of soil.

Ancestor Makes a Negative Confession

Allowances could of course be made,
but the pure intention of the heart
must lay eternally bare before the forty-two Judges.

I have not stopped the flow of water of a neighbor.
I have not pried into others' matters.
I have not stolen the property of God.
I have not caused anyone to weep.
I have not eaten the heart.

Etymologies

God

Neter (Egyptian)—possibly "God"
Nute (Coptic)—possibly "God"

The specific meaning of the word, both in its original ancient Egyptian and its Coptic derivative, has been lost, and today scholars are not in agreement on its definition.

Descendant Mourns Akhenaten

A Lesser Hymn to One God

Creator of Sun, sky, sea, and everything
therein. In the sun-disk Aten manifest.

They who traded in superstition, banked
usury of the destitute and drank sorrow
of the poor, those priests of Amun in the holy
of holies exiled our foremother Nefertiti,
whose sin was loving a loving
man, whose sin was loving a loving
God, his fellow man, creatures of earth,
all matter, the dweller in truth.

But no matter. The One Beyond Time
shines on worthy prophets of any age.
Who is Father and Mother.

Who gives strength needed to love.
Who gives peace beyond reason.

Who gives joy despite knowledge.
Who is worshipped in truth and song.

Who rains on the just and unjust.
Whose light shines without discrimination.

When love is the only law, what matters,
save the content of the heart?

Apophatic Confession

This also is thou; neither is this thou.
—BISHOP KALLISTOS WARE

Long before Lewis wrote, *Taken at their word*
all prayers blaspheme,

before the plaque was erected
to the unknown God,

Akhenaten received his visions,
relocated the capitol, and changed his name.

What else could a man do who had been visited
with the enormity of truth out of time, but reason

the Sun-disk is You; neither
is the Sun-disk You, long before John

the Golden Mouth wrote,
For Thou art God ineffable,

inconceivable, invisible,
incomprehensible, ever-existing,

and even to a heretic pharaoh
centuries before the Incarnation,
eternally the same.

To Become One of the Blessed Dead

Water-purified she stands,
mouth and eyes in her hand, and

hands her heart over to be weighed.
It must exactly balance the scales.

It must exactly equal the weight of Truth.
Heavier, and her heart becomes food for Ammut.

Does her heart pound on cold metal,
awaiting judgement, pulsing

across the single feather of Ma'at, awaiting truth but
fearing justice while Thoth records the result?

Anubis proclaims *her heart is an*
accurate witness. Osiris bids Anubis

give her her eyes and mouth since
her heart is an accurate witness.

The Great Death is nonexistence
if you happen to be beheaded
or your name on earth forgotten
or your heart heavy
or—

II

Question

What becomes of the soul
whose body is unearthed
whose body is eaten?

Etymologies

Mummy

Mumiya (Persian)—bitumen, medicinal

This is not the first nor will it be the last truth
lost in tragic mistranslation. Is it easier, perhaps, to not ask
after proper pronunciation of every foreign-looking name,
send whatever interpreter you have on hand,
or none at all? Mistranslation is, after all, just another
arena, this time on the battlefield of language,
ignoring and neglecting the gleaming weapons,
silence and erasure the grave robbers that pocket
the jewels in the final forgetting.

Mummia (Latin)—human remains (*mistranslation of the Persian*)
Mummy (English)—human remains (*mistranslation of the Persian*)

Mummy Eaters

Was the xiphoid given
due process?

And how long does Ka, Spirit,
travel Duat, land of the dead,
through twelve gates and fire lakes,
speaking secret names of demons,
before she grips the hand of Anubis
in the Hall of Two Truths,
while heart and feather hang together,
weighty with unspeakable deeds?

Does Ka recall the rapidity
of decomposition, feel the press of time,
knowing she must race lest
light-hearted, she reach A'aru to find
she cannot recognize her face?

Mummification being, after all,
the buying of a little time.

And do mummy eaters consider, while
unpermitted gouty fingers sift grave dust,
separate finger from palm, wrist, brew
bone dust tinctures against their excesses?

Do they consider Ka searching,
having made the Negative Confession
before the forty-two Judges, having been weighed
and found worthy,
searching the faces of the dead for her face?
Do they consider—

Immigration

"King (Deceased)"

The French passport read, issued
the disintegrating body of Ramesses II,
the Great who, preserved centuries, began to
really rot in the Egyptian Museum.

North to South: Expedition   Excavation

Said Giovanni Belzoni, *My weight bore on the body of an Egyptian,*
crushed it like a band box. I sunk among broken mummies with a crash,
bones, rags, wooden cases every step I took, I crushed a mummy.

As there is no "mummy" category,
pharaohs traveling north
were once taxed as salted fish.

Said Giovanni Belzoni, *I could not avoid being covered, legs, arms, heads*
rolling from above.
The purpose of my researches was to rob Egyptians of papyri, which I found
hidden in breasts, under arms, above knees.

To save Ramesses II, even he, of the four
seventy-foot statues of himself,
of Abu Simbel, the Golden Age,
enthroned beside Nefertari, he, even he

South to North: Show us your passport.

Living Mummies

It is said Sokushinbutsu is closed to all
but those ten years from death.
For three years the monk eats naught
but nuts, seeds, until lean and hard
he transitions to bark and roots of pine,
his body drying to a husk.

Sap of the urushi tree used as varnish
is now sipped as poisonous tea
while he sweats, pisses, and vomits
all remaining water, locks himself
in a tomb with a slit for air,
and ringing a bell, begins to chant.

Consider my grandmothers revolving.
Circles contracting, options, like time, dwindling,
slowing, hardening, joints and thoughts petrifying,
walls tightening brick by brick, opening
into vast stillness and the endless hereafter.

The monks know to seal the tomb
when the bell ceases to ring.

A Dealer Sits

A dealer sits nodding off
beside what he could find
that colonizer valued,
like any farmer
at the mercy of soil's harvest.

Impoverished or pimp:
What choice is there?

Several mummified
bodies stand propped
against a mud-brick wall,
one leans back,

head tilted,
slumped in sleep.
Is anyone awake here?

Flesh Trade

From Cairo to Alexandria to Europe
traffic flows in a parade of bones:
xiphoid, sacrum, tibia, fibula.

Lest anyone misunderstand,
Egyptians also, to feed their hungry children,
fed strange appetites of those they could not
understand, dug up treasures they could not
understand, their ancestors, the left legacy
preserved, human remains.

Buyer beware, counterfeits abound.
Careful lest you purchase
camel, ibis, or corpse of
recently departed British criminals,
as when embalmed we creatures
tend to look alike.

Fibula, tibia, sacrum, xiphoid,
sold up the Nile for a half-dirham.

Descendants Discuss Motivation, Your Honor

They said ground mummy skull could cure
the European headache. Parts for gout, European hysteria.

Parts to ease labor, or cure even a lack of
love. Mummy: the ultimate aphrodisiac.

It is said mummy contained power,
a strong life force, that of the rich dead,

life force of a strong people guarded
by a now-poor, *ignorant*

and superstitious people, said Belzoni,
a primitive nation.

Ripe, ripe, ripe for the unearthing.
People poor enough to sell their

—follow the money—ancestors
out of the earth beneath their feet.

Descendants Discuss Literary Merits of Mummy Eating

What part of a person eats another?
Dorian Gray eyes his murdered friend,

thinks *the secret of the whole thing*
was not to realize the situation.

His human remains an object, names his friend
the dead thing. Macbeth's witches cackle,

Double double toil and trouble
Fire burn and cauldron bubble.

Do the three witches exist, or just
in the mind of a troubled poet or king?

Adding, along with *scale of dragon, tooth of*
wolf, eye of newt, the witches' mummy.

Marlow said he was *becoming scientifically*
interesting and I believe I am becoming

dangerously close to the Heart
of Darkness, wherein, by the way,

is Europe the protagonist and Africa
the antagonist or is it the other way

around? And what part of a person eats
another other than the mind?

Thomas Pettigrew Mansplains Mummies

Before becoming founding treasurer
of the British Archeological Society
—Was there ever a greater irony?—
he gave pontificating lectures
in sold out events, exercised his talents
as antiquarian and surgeon.

For entertainment of guests,
he unrolled dead human remains
propped in palms of volunteers.
He unrolled linen,
onlookers marveling, *so much linen*.
Clouds of white-yellow stained linen,
mountains of it rose
until the small, dried body emerged,
much smaller, vulnerable,
more naked than expected.

It is said he aimed to prove
Egyptians were Caucasian
using cranial measurements.
They're just like us, you see?

Powerful Ancients all alien,
dark, wise, foreign-looking.
Terrible and beautiful, *but look,*
stripped bare we have restored
balance to power.

Isn't it difficult to fear
what you've unwrapped?
Dark specters banished.
The violated swatted back down
in their place once more.

How to Silence I

British Lessons

At the summit of arrogance, Britain,
to protect her interests, the Suez Canal being
strategically placed, occupied Egypt.

What a polite word, *occupy*. It isn't
in your best interest to be interesting
to the wrong people.

Did we learn the lesson?

A Coptic monk watches workers
cover with plaster an ancient apse.
When asked if he knew the value

of what they were covering he replied:
Our quiet, sacred space an attraction
for restorers, experts, tourists.

Of course we know the value
of our heritage. That is why
we are covering it up, he smiled.

How to Silence II

Roman Lessons

There are only two guarantees.
Well versed in the language
of their conquered, to thwart those
who would thwart taxation, Romans
held mummies ransom.

Preinterred dead, propped up
presiding over evening meals, participating
in daily life while their Ka made its way through Duat.
Families felt no rush really
to inter they who were seeking eternal rest.

The body of the beloved biding with family,
who took comfort, holding on a while longer
until graceless Roman fingers entered
the private mysterious balance
between life and death and

let the dead remain unburied
until the living raised enough money
to unlock the ground, to remind
the conquered who they were,
and who they were.

Stolen Hour

I grip her hand above the worst bruising.
Lines all came out with the DNR order.

Her fingers are cold but her palm warm and
mine curl in shelter there, taking.

Even in brain death her nails are nicer than mine.
She would've told me so too, and I grip harder while

silent tears wet the bedspread, waiting for mom
to come back from the funeral home.

Someone has filled in the names of her doctor,
nurse, nurse's aide, next of kin. The only name missing

is hers. Malaka Hanna, Queen, I write,
close my eyes, pray the prayer of the sick,

the dying, and the dead, and she is eyeing me
from the head of the bed. I blink and she is shrugging

into her jacket by the door, rifling through her purse, and
painting on an unapologetic layer of red lipstick.

Y'alla, she says, heels clacking past the nurses,
her crown of white hair regal in the breeze,

windows down as we drive home. On the radio
Umm Kulthūm is belting "Enta Omri."

She eyes her ring on my finger and says, *Your nails
need doing*, and I agree through salty tears.

We air out the musty apartment and she rests,
winded, a glass of mango juice in hand.

Well? she asks, *What do you need? I was on my way,
but you needed something*, and waits while I snivel,

listen to the fourteen clocks ticktock seconds apart and
desperately review her life. She raised sisters,

her own children dead of typhoid, ran an orphanage,
became famous for her Lebanese Greek cooking, infamous

for her mysterious second husband. She immigrated,
persisted, despite an entire family's disapproval.

"How do you like yourself so much?" I ask.
"Confidently, not caring what they all think,

not needing their approval?" and she nods knowingly.
Khodee bal'ik min nafs'ik, she says. *Take care of your*

Self, and I close my eyes and rest my head.
Nafs: self but also soul, soul near to breath.

Despite comfort care settings monitors are beeping,
her tongue swollen beneath the breathing tube.

An hour after extubation they will search for a magnet
to destroy the pacemaker mistakenly placed

after sending an Arabic-speaking woman a Spanish
interpreter, but for now, we sit together and breathe.

How to Silence III

Greek Lessons

He squints during the chanting,
a guest in our service. *Agios O Theos,*
Holy God, we pray, Holy Mighty, Holy Immortal.
"Oh," he says. "You're trying to speak Greek here!"
In his eyes I see the word *bastardization*.

Behind it, *monophysite*, and behind that,
the failure of Dioscorus, the councils, the exclusion,
the seating of a foreign patriarch on domestic soil, and
the inevitable rewriting of history by the victor.

In his veins echo the cold of Alexander, Great to some.
And on my brow rests the heavy crown of Cleopatra,
who used all her power, including her womb,
to ward off the invading horde.
Except she was Greek too.

And it is the Popular Patristics bio
of Saint Athanasius all over again.
Egyptian by birth, Greek by education.
No sign of national consciousness, nor does he
display the Coptic temperament.

Race against Time II

They would rather believe Aliens
built Pyramids

—not the Parthenon
    not the Colosseum—

than admit Brown and Black people
built what they cannot explain,

than admit Brown and Black people
built what withstands time.

Mummy Brown

Dead man's head, worthless remains.
Egyptian Brown, that Fugitive Color
between burnt and raw umber
the pre-Raphaelites favored for
flesh tones and shadows

flows from the brush with
delightful freedom.

Recipe: white pitch, myrrh and ground
cat and human remains.

Edward Burne-Jones, repulsed
when he discovered the origins,
buried his tube of Mummy Brown
ceremoniously in the garden, easy-like

it's easy—like when you find the land
you thought yours wasn't
or empire built by enslaved people—
Bury it—

He didn't take down the paintings, mind.
He just buried the last tube among the petunias.

Supply and Demand

I

A Found Poem from eBay

"collector   Pharaonic Antique

gather   from many places
gather   from original owner

information   collected
                from original owner

Items   legally

acquired   Legitimate Sources."

II

A London colorman
bemoaned in 1915
that he could meet the demand

of his customers
for twenty years with
—follow the money—
a single mummy.

III

Race against Time III

Never go to an Egyptian funeral
late.

Weddings, sure. An hour late
they're still wreathing the church.

But a funeral, get you to the church early
because by a quarter till
there's no parking,
church crammed to the walls,
a sea of somber black, because

They respect the dead,
my father says,
more than the living.

Descendant Talks Suffering with Old Aunties

Old Aunties always said the wrong-right thing
in the right-wrong spirit, at the wrong-wrong time.

Your eyebrows are bushy, your laugh
too loud, also you could still stand to lose
a few pounds, and if you wait longer
the good men will be gone, but if you study longer
you'll be unmarriageable, though you're still young.
You can always try for another baby.

Suffering, Basil the Great said, *makes
a person so sensitive that he becomes like an eye
which cannot bear even the touch of a feather.*

Descendant Opening of the Eyes

A Daughter's Long Wail

Mish bi'tiwgah einik?
Does this not hurt your eyes?
my mother asks and she means
messes,
room disarrayed, laundry upturned,
books on every surface. She means
bed unmade, dishes unwashed.
She means
it should hurt your eyes, if you look.

She means, if you see a mess,
you should clean it up.

Ya Omi, They dug us up.
Ate us, *ya Omi.*
Painted with our powdered bones,
mixed us into a palate to make flesh tones.
Their
flesh tones, *ya Omi.*

Burned us to fertilize their crops,
to eat us again, *ya Omi.*
Paper we became for them to write their lies upon,
ya Omi, while our language unravels
like yards
and yards of stained linen, *ya Omi.*

Mish bi'tiwgah einik?
Yes, it hurts
my eyes, *ya Omi,*
it hurts.

Descendant Interrogated about Suffering and Ancestry

But how do you know she belongs
to you?

Where are you *from*
from?

I don't, and I'll tell you.

At the trailhead we unload our bikes.
Teenagers yell from a distance,
Go back to Mexico.

It's no use yelling back.
They've never left home.

Yelling only works on listening
ears, pouring onto open pages
of a heart spine-split like a book.

Stop yelling. Listen.
Allow us to school you
on how we bind and heal, negotiate
and calculate the fate
of the free world.

Though we look brown to you,
it would be more accurate to tell us
—descendants of Ancients—
to go back to Africa,
because my ancestors had the circumference of the earth

approximated long before
yours tried to cross the sea looking to claim a New World.

But then
    at this distance

it's hard to tell
    who your ancestors were.

Descendant Addresses French Boy

Skin Politics

In Mumbai they ask
if I'm Aishwarya Rai.
If you run for office, they counsel,
you're light-skinned enough to win.

What the French left behind:
infrastructure and blue-green-eyed bastards.
What they took, among unspoken things:
the brown of our eyes and skin, though
they do like their eyes above our lips,
framed by the coarseness of our hair.

Like Indians, cricket, Great Britain,
I take your French-boy eyes
and play them better.

If I score, I'm French, says Karim Benzema.
If I don't, I'm Arab.

In the souks in Cairo they sell
bleaching creams and my mother
tells me to *stay out of the sun* not
because melanoma, but because men
prefer pale skin like they prefer colored eyes.
Dear French boy: I want back
the brown you stole.

Descendants Offer Prayer

MATHER OF GOD PRY
FOR US shouts the handwritten
sign in block letters, pegged to the bumper
of a truck bed piled high with bricks,
sides unsupported. A man sits atop,
while we all sit choking on traffic exhaust.

How can you expect a people,
tongues taken for praying, to articulate
the depths of their need?

Etymologies

Book of the Dead

> Wretched people, toiling people, do not play . . . In Egypt the
> center of interest was the dead.
> —EDITH HAMILTON

They say we are obsessed with death,
actions sarcophagus oriented,
days spent preparing for mummification,
navigating with death as our North Star.
We, who have no word for death,
for ceasing to exist? No, Edith, no.

See the scarab that rolls the sun
through the night, over the horizon
where it is reborn every morning.
See the lotus that rises from River murk.
Look upon good deeds done in the bright
light of eternity and understand.

There is no *this* life, then *that*.
There is one path beneath our feet
with a death-rimmed horizon,
one tapestry woven by the weaving Hand,
though some threads be invisible.
We navigate by the Resurrection of the dead.

There is no death, we chant,
unto thy servant, but a departure.
The Book of the Dead a mistranslation
for the Book of Going Forth into Morning,
for the Book of Emerging Forth into the Light.
Tell me again who is obsessed with death?

Is it an obsession with death, or
a rightful preoccupation with the eternal,
continuous life of the soul?
Keep your mind in Hell,
said Silouan, *and despair not,* of this
undammed River, flowing from life to life.

Cairo, 1958

Siblings before complications, they dangle
spindly legs in the high balcony, cracking

salted watermelon seeds between their teeth,
spitting down into the alley.

Their latest batch lay shimmering, drying
in the windowsill when the building collapsed

next door, all three stories crumbling to dust.
Three stories full of human stories crumbling

to dust, fine white dust rising and coating
their legs, dust rising like a cough

in young lungs, dust rising and ruining.
They were warned to move, she says, hands

swirling wash water. *The building swayed
but they were too poor to move, and we were too little,*

she shrugs, *to be upset about anything
other than our watermelon seeds.*

Descendants Discuss Definitives

The age-old question: What is the difference
between a pirate and a privateer?

If you sell crack or take it to dull the pain,
they call you crackhead and incarcerate you.

If you prescribe opium to dull the pain,
they call you doctor and thank you.

If you pay cash so employees keep subsidized housing,
they call you tax evader and incarcerate you.

If you build empires on the backs of people who get no tax breaks on
    rent,
they call you Mr. President and salute you.

If you take bread for your hungry children,
they call you thief and incarcerate you.

If you *own* the largest collection of stolen goods on earth
they call you [*Encyclopedic*] Museum—

Descendant Names Modern Mummy Eaters

We are much more progressive now.
We politely unravel displaced mummies in

sanitized basements of [*Encyclopedic*] Museums,
untuck their amulets and number them.

During the 1926–1927 excavation season . . .
299 scarabs . . . sixty-five in Museum, Cairo,

the rest acquired by the [Encyclopedic] *Museum*
in the division of finds.

We gobble them with our eyes beside CT scans
of their insides in a civilized cybernetic unwrapping,

these spoils of innumerable wars, now under lock and alarm,
where none witness—save those with a passport—

the extent of thievery in this courteous
cabinet of [*Encyclopedic*] curiosities.

Numbers

Dad hands her the hard pit of a complex
math problem, then pulls up the covers.
Mom, thinking it would take but a moment,
turns on a night-light to begin.
It is past three a.m. when she gives up.
Later, he delights in solving it aloud,
a magician, revealing hat lining.
It's simple, he says, *you need strategy.*

math strategy: *During the 1926–1927 excavation season . . .
299 scarabs . . . sixty-five in Museum, Cairo,*

the rest acquired by the [Encyclopedic] *Museum
in the division of finds.*

Over half a century ago,
great-grandmother Fayza,
unable to count, hands full of dates,
looks down into the upturned faces
of her five grandchildren, slips one date
into each upturned palm, then begins again.
Palm, date, palm, date, one after another
until her hands are empty.

How to Silence

Mathematics Edition

He has finally after thirty-nine years
sold the station that paid school fees,

Velcro shoes, countless Pee-Chee
folders, the used bulbous Toyota,

the mortgage. When I ask him
how he feels he describes bitter sweetness

of retiring, of no longer belonging to
the thing that belonged to him so long

she felt more mistress than business.
His clearest memory: hunched over a text-

book studying non-Euclidean geometry
between clients after 9/11, a man

he knew asking between the
hyperbolic and the spherical, *What?*

Are you studying to be a pilot?
Baba's mute stare, unable to muster

any reply, like a landed fish.
After the limit, he describes

the joy felt in the midst of pure
mathematics, proofs, definitions.

Between the point and the plane,
lines and assumptions, then the assumption.

Being yanked out of his pride into the gutter
of another man's question until the man finally

cried, *Eddie*—my father's real
name is Ragaa—*oh, come on!*

True Mirror

It is said if you saw your face as others see,
you would hardly recognize your-*self*.
Mirror shows reflection, not truth.
Dimly we see head tilt, asymmetry
of eyes and nose. Would we tilt our heads
to the wrong side, then brow furrowed,
pass ourselves by? Did a single soul
in all the passage of time—did Ancestor—ever recognize
the body, the face, she left behind?

Ancestor Calms Descendant's Fears about Having Children in a World without Kemet

But plague.

> There will always be plague of one sort or another.

But soil is brittle and dry. Nothing grows but Progress.

> Soil is forgiving. Though the whole earth be soil after the Dam, God will send another Inundation.

But people are unkind.

> They aren't, they aren't. Mobs are unkind, people are not.

But danger.   We cannot cross lines on maps without permission because of the color of our skin and the language of our ancestors.

> God hears in all language, and in the void of language.

But time.   It feels like the end, doesn't it?

> Though the world end in poverty and plague tomorrow, yet must you plant seeds today, quality of the soil be damned.

El Asar

In Luxor, a hungry Coptic girl digs
in dry earth beneath her pallet
for *Asar*, ancestry,
hoping for a gleam of dull
burnished gold, anything
that can be converted to food.

Omi says the stealing of artifacts
is in Egypt's best interest, but do countries
have interests?

Of what use is Asar, Baba asks,
when it just sits in the ground?

How to Silence IV

Arabic Lessons

Sister, when our mother woke after surgery,
breast abscess excised, unable to nurse,

nearly losing her life, Baba across oceans,
her Muslim sisters divvied her call shifts.

When she woke scared, one sat beside her
rocking and praying the Koran.

Hurt ones entreat me to tell tales of tongue slashers,
permits to fix toilets in crumbling churches, permits

requiring presidential signatures. *To relieve ourselves,*
Presidential signatures, they wail.

They tell tales of hands that rip crosses from necks,
spray backs of churches with bullets.

Those are not tales, they are true but
truer still and more urgent is the tale of our mother.

I ask you, What need have we of persecuted minorities
in one country calling out persecuted minorities

in another country? And would it help if hatred
bred hatred, or instead of giving airtime to cross rippers,

could we pray ourselves awake chanting of God
in whatever tongue left to us? I will rock over you,

sister (whatever you do with your hair:
braid it, curl it, cover it, or shave it),

rock over you chanting *Ekowab*.
You will rock over me chanting *Bismillah*.

And we will rock and chant together
until these nations find their tongues, until the soil

black once more and the River twist liberated,
dancing into the mouth of the sea.

Ou-ta

How to Speak from Silence

He is still earning his land legs,
his walk the sway of a sailor on leave.
His tongue forms all of seven words,
one of which is *ou-ta*. His tongue ripens the Coptic
emphasis on the *ou*, the ringing *ta*.
How does a tongue that has never tasted tomatoes
in the motherland somehow absorb syllables
of a language nearly gone from the earth,
spoken aloud for centuries until it was slashed
out of the mouths of our ancestors?
This little word, tiny as a tomato seed,
sprouted into the Arabic, handed down
in its roundness and rightness from mouth to mouth
in the colloquial until at last, my infant son,
across continents can squat beside the summer-heavy vine,
grasp the red fullness in his tiny fist, and babble
back into the language of Ancients.

Final Test

After the weighing of hearts,
before the Field of Reeds,

before A'aru, Soul of the Great River,
tomb behind, ahead Sun rise, perfect

mirror of life, toil pleasant, harvest
plentiful, soil fertile, eternal flax

to spin into eternal linen, music of grain,
abundant breeze laden with figs and honey,

beyond memory, after the death of death,
before the new God-given name,

in the absence of pain, every body
in its prime, before love without loss,

she walks a ways along the path to the
Lake of Lilies, to the shore where surly

Heref-Haef, Divine Ferryman, awaits eternally disagreeable.
Mother, sister, daughter, there is no other way across.

In the face of his arbitrary injustice, *unnecessary*,
you will want to say, *Who are you anyway?*

My heart has already been weighed. But don't.
Though unpleasant, one must find a way

to be pleasant to him. Courtesy
in the face of bald injustice is the final test.

Letters for My Grandmothers

A giantess is stirring onions into the sixteen
thousand four hundred and twenty-fifth meal.

She knows no more of letters
than the slanted slash of signature,
unknown characters strung and memorized,
as illiterate of Arabic as I.

Fouziya slides a gold bangle down a thick arm
to buy a copper tub to celebrate the birth
of a grandson twice seen.
Married old at twenty-one, she pries her ring off
to pay rent and groceries. *Take this*, she tells him.
Are we not still married? You can buy me another
when we have money, knowing there would never be
either money or another.

Nadra, beaded sweat over frying fish,
steaming cabbage and broiling beef,
vanquishes spinach with a two-handled blade.
She buys me a necklace that reads *Taurus*
though I am a Pisces because
she thinks it reads *I love you*.

I imagine the physicist,
immunologist, concert pianist,
hidden in the heart of the giantess
stirring onions at the stove.

It is meal sixteen thousand four hundred
and twenty-five of twice that many
and she no less worthy than I
of learning her letters.

NOTES AND REFERENCES

MUMMIFICATION: EARLY LESSONS
Italicized lines are from the Book of the Dead, translated by E. A. Wallis Budge (1898).

SHABTI, USHABTI: "ANSWERER"
Italicized line is from the Book of the Dead, translated by E. A. Wallis Budge (1898).

ANCESTOR MAKES A NEGATIVE CONFESSION
Italicized lines are from the Negative Confession, Papyrus of Ani (240 BCE), from the Book of the Dead, translated by E. A. Wallis Budge (1898).

ETYMOLOGIES: GOD
Italicized lines are from Jill Kamil, *Christianity in the Land of the Pharaohs: The Coptic Orthodox Church* (London: Routledge, 2002).

TO BECOME ONE OF THE BLESSED DEAD
Italicized lines are from the Tomb of Meritamun (TT 358, MMA 65), first corridor, inside Osiris figure, MMA excavations, 1928–29, *The Singer of Amun Nany's Funerary Papyrus*, ca. 1050 BC, Metropolitan Museum of Art, https://www.metmuseum.org/art/collection/search/545191.

IMMIGRATION: "KING (DECEASED)"
Italicized portions quoted from Giovanni Battista Belzoni, *Narrative of the Operations and Recent Discoveries within the Pyramids, Temples, Tombs, and Excavations, in Egypt and Nubia* (Egypt: 1835).

DESCENDANTS DISCUSS MOTIVATION, YOUR HONOR
Italicized portions quoted from Giovanni Battista Belzoni, *Narrative of the Operations and Recent Discoveries within the Pyramids, Temples, Tombs, and Excavations, in Egypt and Nubia* (Egypt: 1835).

HOW TO SILENCE III: GREEK LESSONS
Italicized portions are from *The Life of St. Athanasius*, preceding the text of "On the Incarnation," translated and edited by a religious of CMSV (New York: St Vladimir's Seminary Press, 1996).

MUMMY BROWN
The portion in italics is quoted by Heather Pringle in *The Mummy Congress: Science, Obsession, and the Everlasting Dead* (New York: Hyperion, 2001), but the source quotation is unidentified.

ETYMOLOGIES: BOOK OF THE DEAD
The epigraph is from Edith Hamilton, *The Greek Way* (New York: W. W. Norton, 1942).

"There is no death unto thy servant, but a departure" is from the Coptic Liturgy of St. Basil the Great.

DESCENDANT NAMES MODERN MUMMY EATERS and NUMBERS
Italicized description of scarab discovery and acquisition is from *Scarabs from Hatshepsut Foundation Deposits*, ca. 1479–1458 BC, Metropolitan Museum of Art, https://www.metmuseum.org/art/collection/search/559804.

New-Generation African Poets:
A Chapbook Box Set (Nne)
Edited by Kwame Dawes
and Chris Abani
(Akashic Books)

New-Generation African Poets:
A Chapbook Box Set (Saba)
Edited by Kwame Dawes
and Chris Abani
(Akashic Books)

New-Generation African Poets:
A Chapbook Box Set (Tano)
Edited by Kwame Dawes
and Chris Abani
(Akashic Books)

New-Generation African Poets:
A Chapbook Box Set (Nane)
Edited by Kwame Dawes
and Chris Abani
(Akashic Books)

New-Generation African Poets:
A Chapbook Box Set (Sita)
Edited by Kwame Dawes
and Chris Abani
(Akashic Books)

To order or obtain more information on these or other University of
Nebraska Press titles, visit nebraskapress.unl.edu. For more information
about the African Poetry Book Series, visit africanpoetrybf.unl.edu.

Printed in the USA
CPSIA information can be obtained
at www.ICGtesting.com
CBHW021445190224
4471CB00002B/82

9 781496 232540